Let's Trace Straight Lines

To Parents: This activity is designed to teach how to draw lines from top to bottom. Have your child use a crayon, marker, or pencil depending on his or her abilities.

The cars are moving very fast. Trace the ▪▪▪▪ from ➡ to ➡.

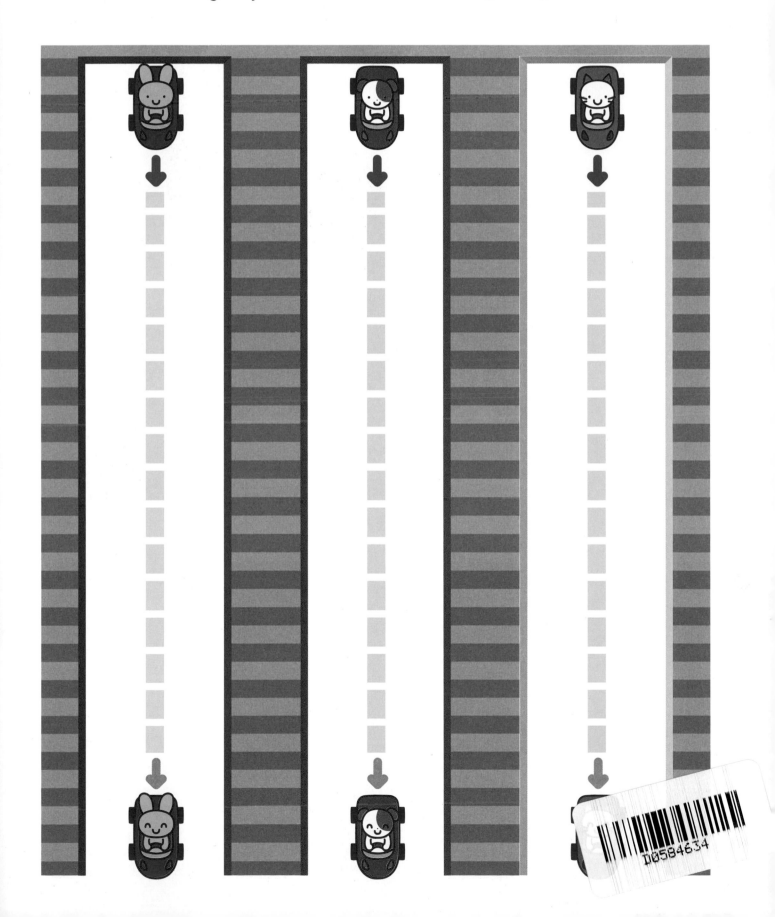

2

Let's Trace Zigzag Lines

To Parents: In this activity, your child will practice drawing zigzag lines. Have your child stop at each bend to change directions.

GOOD JOB!

Sticker

Let's drive to the station. Trace the ▪▪▪▪ from ➡ to ➡.

Let's Trace Curved Lines

To Parents: This activity is designed to teach how to draw curves. After your child has finished drawing, have him or her use the stickers from the front of the book to complete the activity.

Turtle and Penguin swim through the water. Trace the ▰▰▰▰ from ➡ to ➡.

Place the 🐢 and 🐧 stickers on ⌐Sticker⌐.

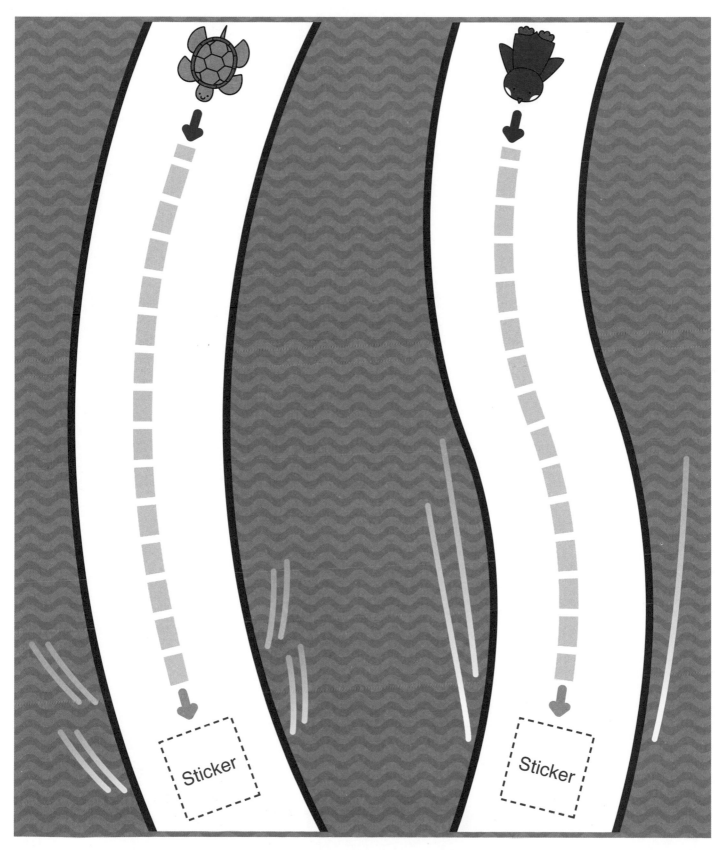

4

Let's Draw Lines

To Parents: Encourage your child to draw from the pink arrows to the blue arrows in one continuous stroke.

The birds are flying in the sky. Trace the ▰▰▰ from ➡ to ➡.

Place the 🐦 and 🐦 stickers on ┊Sticker┊.

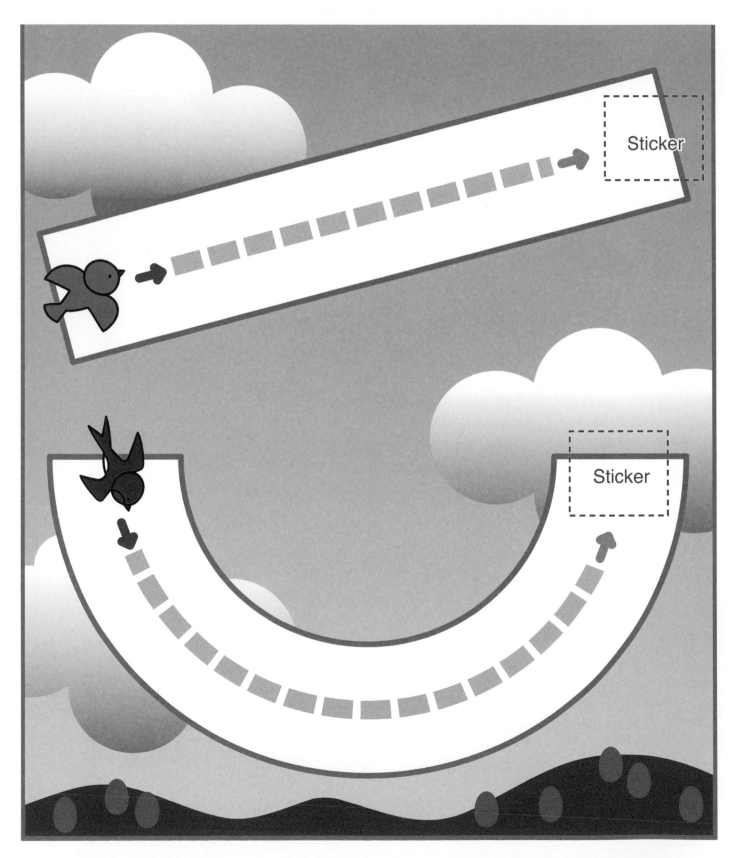

Let's Draw Curves

To Parents: In this activity, your child will practice drawing lines that start out straight and then become curvy. Drawing straight-to-curvy lines helps build strong handwriting skills.

5

The animals are running a race. Trace the ▬▬▬ from ➡ to ➡.

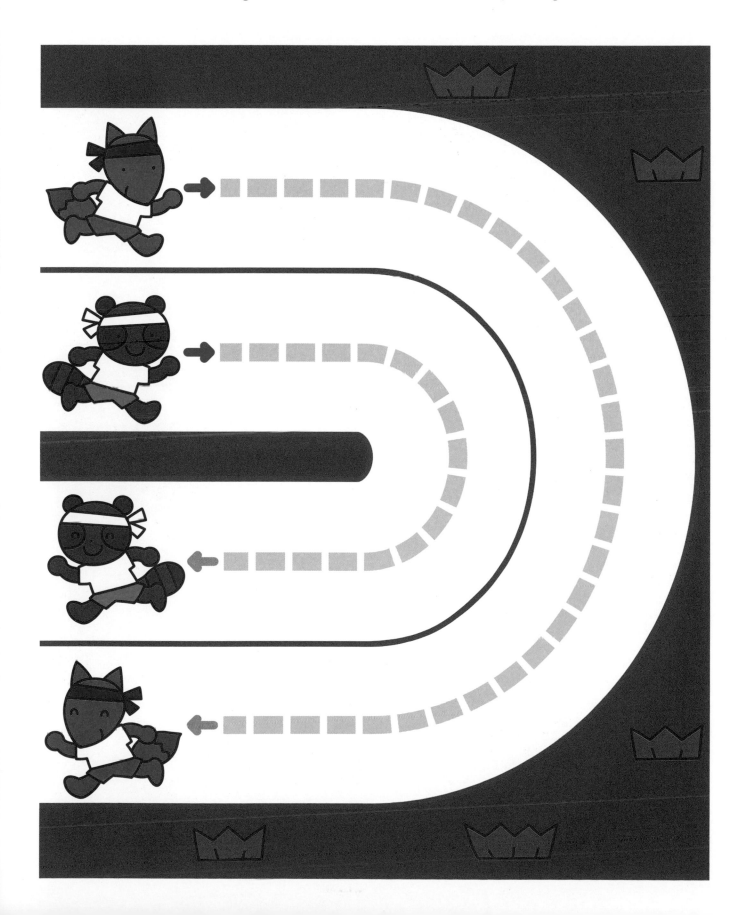

Let's Draw Lines

To Parents: This activity focuses on drawing a straight line that changes direction. This can be difficult. Encourage your child to work slowly and to pause at each corner before making the sharp turn.

The animals are playing soccer. Trace the ▰▰▰ from ➡ to ➡.

Let's Draw Curves

GOOD JOB!

Sticker

Giraffe and Pig are playing catch. Trace the from to .

8

Let's Draw Zigzags

To Parents: This activity focuses on drawing zigzag lines from left to right and from right to left.

The birds go back to their nest. Trace the ▬▬ from ➡ to ➡.

Let's Trace Arcs

To Parents: In this activity, your child will practice drawing a series of consecutive arcs. Make sure your child stops at the end of each arc before moving on to the next.

Grasshopper and Frog are jumping over the flowers. Trace the ▰▰▰▰

from ➡ to ➡. Place the 🦗 and 🐸 stickers on Sticker.

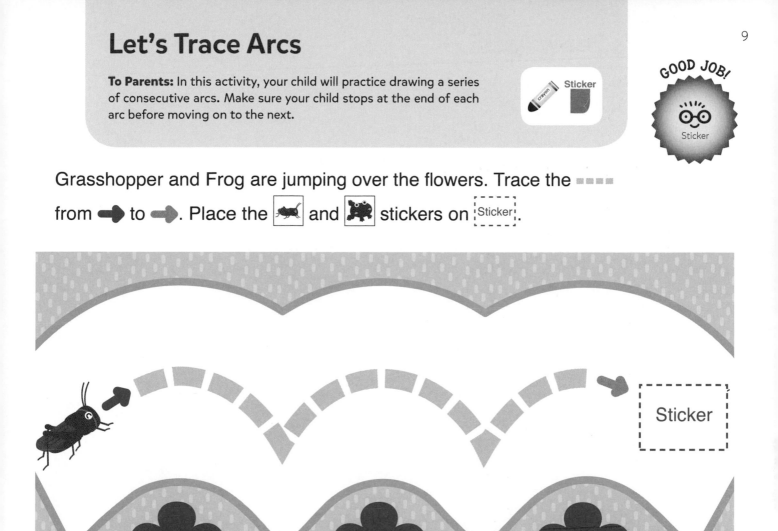

Let's Draw Arcs

To Parents: Here, your child will practice drawing arcs. Being able to draw an arc is a step toward drawing a circle.

Bird is flying, and Fish is swimming. Trace the ▪▪▪▪ from ➡ to ➡.

Let's Draw A Circle

To Parents: This activity is designed to teach your child how to draw a circle. This may be hard for your child. He or she may stray outside the dotted line. That is okay. Your child will get better with practice.

GOOD JOB!

Sticker

The rocket is circling Earth. Trace the ▪▪▪▪ from ➡ to ➡.

Let's Draw a Loop

To Parents: In this activity, your child will draw a loop, where the end of the line crosses over the beginning of the line. Encourage your child to draw using a single, quick stroke, like a roller coaster looping around.

GOOD JOB!
Sticker

The roller coaster loops around. The roller coaster is very fast!

Trace the ▬▬▬ from ➡ to ➡.

Let's Trace a Shape

To Parents: The shape in this activity is made up of several different types of lines (short, long, straight, curved). Encourage your child to pay special attention to each kind of line.

Let's ride a tricycle around the lake. Trace the ▪▪▪▪ from ➡ to ➡.

14

Let's Trace a Shape

To Parents: The shape in this activity is made up of curved lines and straight lines. Encourage your child to pay special attention to the different kinds of lines.

GOOD JOB!

Sticker

Panda is taking a stroll around the garden. Trace the ▰▰▰▰ from ➡ to ➡.

Let's Match the Animals

To Parents: Ask your child to name each animal (cat, snake, chicken) in the maze below. Then, ask him or her to draw the line that connects the chicken to her chick.

Who is the chick's mother? Trace the ▬ ▬ from ➡ to ➡.

16

Let's Match the Animals

To Parents: Explain that a baby frog is called a tadpole. Then, ask your child to help the tadpole find its mother.

GOOD JOB!

Sticker

Which one is Frog's baby? Trace the ▰▰▰ from ➡ to ➡.

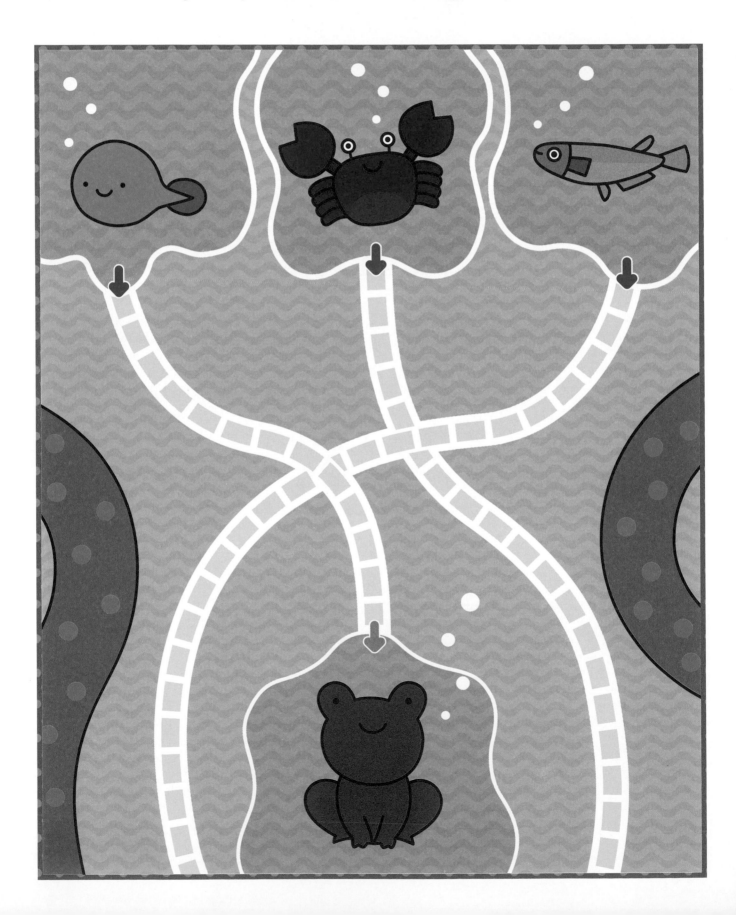

Let's Trace the Lines

To Parents: Before your child begins tracing, ask questions like: "Which food can you eat without silverware?" and "Which foods would you eat with a fork?" Feel free to make up your own questions.

Which animal is eating each dish? Say the name of the animal and the food. Then, trace each ▪▪▪▪ from ➡ to ➡.

Let's Follow the Lines

To Parents: Encourage your child to follow each line with his or her finger before tracing the correct dotted line with a crayon, marker, or pencil.

The hamster is hungry. Which dotted line leads to its food?

Trace the correct  from ➡ to ➡. Place the 🐼 sticker on ⌐Sticker¬.

Sticker

FOOD

Let's Find the Right Path

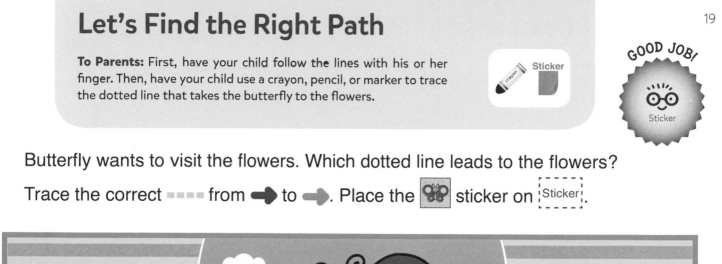

To Parents: First, have your child follow the lines with his or her finger. Then, have your child use a crayon, pencil, or marker to trace the dotted line that takes the butterfly to the flowers.

GOOD JOB!
Sticker

Butterfly wants to visit the flowers. Which dotted line leads to the flowers?

Trace the correct ▪▪▪▪ from ➡ to ➡. Place the 🦋 sticker on ⌐Sticker⌐.

Sticker

20

Let's Draw a Bow

To Parents: This activity is designed to teach shape recognition. Guide your child to draw the shape in one stroke, which helps to build handwriting skills.

GOOD JOB!
Sticker

Let's trace the shape of the bow. Trace the ▬▬▬ from ➡ to ➡.

Let's Draw a Hat

To Parents: This activity Is designed to teach shape recognition. It is also good handwriting practice.

GOOD JOB!
Sticker

Let's trace the shape of the hat. Trace the **----** from ➡ to ➡.

Let's Draw a Star

To Parents: This activity is designed to teach shape recognition. Guide your child to draw the shape in one stroke, which strengthens handwriting skills.

GOOD JOB!
Sticker

Let's trace the shape of the star. Trace the ▰▰▰ from ➡ to ➡.

Let's Draw a Figure Eight

To Parents: Drawing a figure eight allows your child to make circles clockwise and counterclockwise.

Let's trace the shape of the owl's eyes. Trace the ▰▰▰ from ➡ to ➡.

Let's Draw a Dog

To Parents: On this page, the dotted line is only there to get your child started. Encourage your child to continue drawing around the dog without going outside the white path.

GOOD JOB!
Sticker

Let's draw the shape of the dog's head. Draw a line from ➡ to ➡.

Let's Draw a Fish

To Parents: Have your child start drawing on top of the dotted line. Then encourage her or him to continue drawing around the fish and to try to stay within the white path.

GOOD JOB!
Sticker

Let's draw the shape of the big fish. Draw a line from ➡ to ➡.

26

Let's Draw a Boat

GOOD JOB!

Sticker

Let's draw the shape of the boat. Draw a line from ➡ to ➡.

Let's Draw a Flower

To Parents: Drawing shapes of all kinds helps your child build the skills needed for handwriting.

Let's draw the shape of the flower. Draw a line from ➡ to ➡.

Let's Go Through the Maze

To Parents: This is a very simple maze. As the activities progress, the mazes will become more complex. You will find the stickers in the front of the book.

Let's feed the monkeys. For each fruit, draw a line from ➡ to ➡.

Place the fruit stickers on Sticker.

Let's Complete the Maze

To Parents: To get through the maze, your child will need to draw straight lines. Encourage him or her to stop at each intersection before changing directions.

GOOD JOB!
Sticker

Let's help the puppy and kitten find their mothers. Draw lines from each ➡ to ➡.

Then, place the 🐶 and 🐱 stickers on the Sticker boxes.

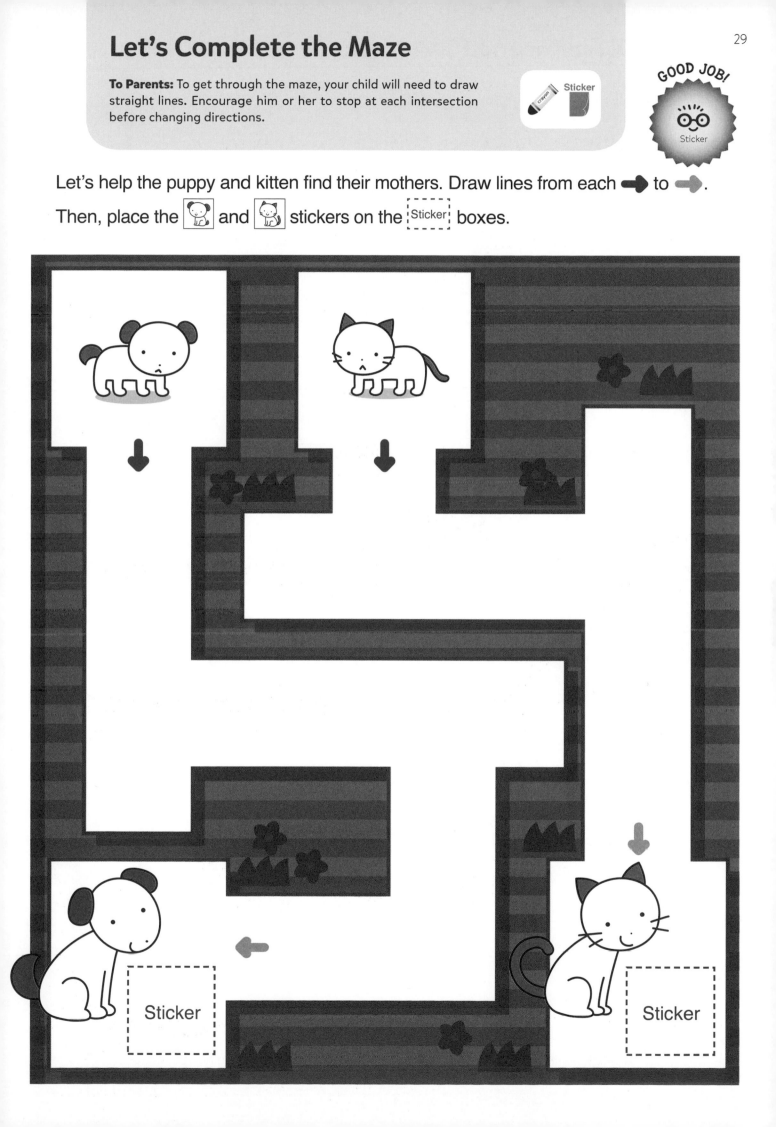

Let's Follow the Path

To Parents: In this maze, one path leads to the garden and one path leads to a dead end. It is important for your child to stop and look at each path option before deciding which way to go.

GOOD JOB!
Sticker

Let's help Rabbit water the flowers. Draw a line from ➡ to ➡.

Let's Go Through the Maze

To Parents: Before your child draws on the maze, encourage him or her to determine whether each lily pad is connected to the maze. After your child has finished the maze, have him or her put the frog sticker on the lily pad Frog reaches.

GOOD JOB!
Sticker

Let's help Frog find her favorite lily pad.

Draw a line from ➡ to ➡. Place the 🐸 sticker on the ⬤.

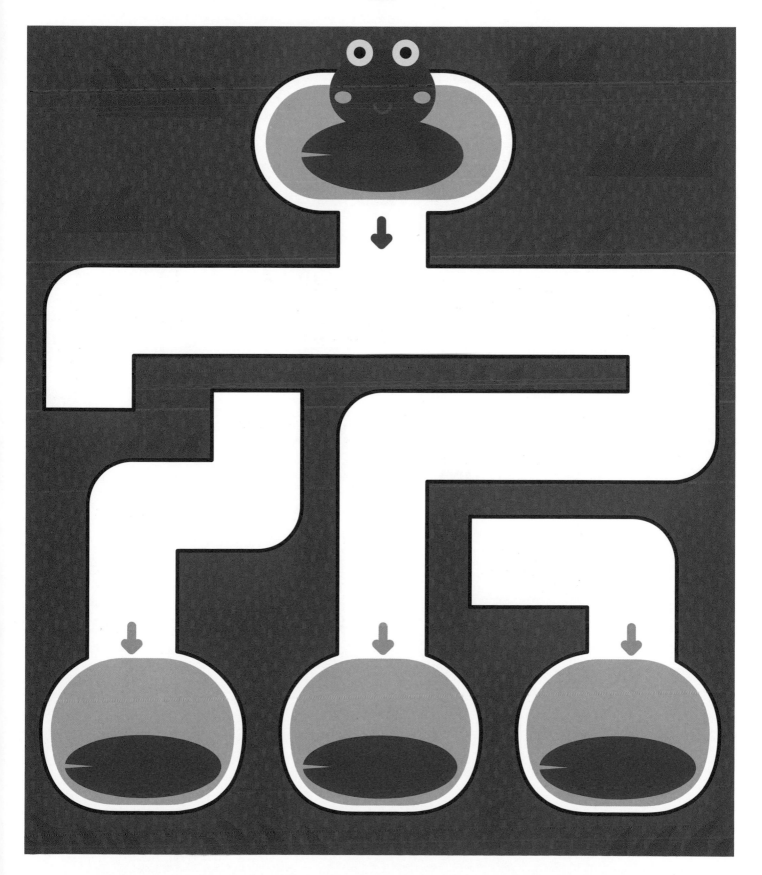

Let's Find the Right Way to Go

To Parents: Using a crayon, marker, or pencil to do mazes helps to build handwriting skills.

Sticker

GOOD JOB!
Sticker

Let's help Squirrel find his house.

Draw a line from ➡ to ➡. Place the 🐿 sticker on ⬜ at the correct house.

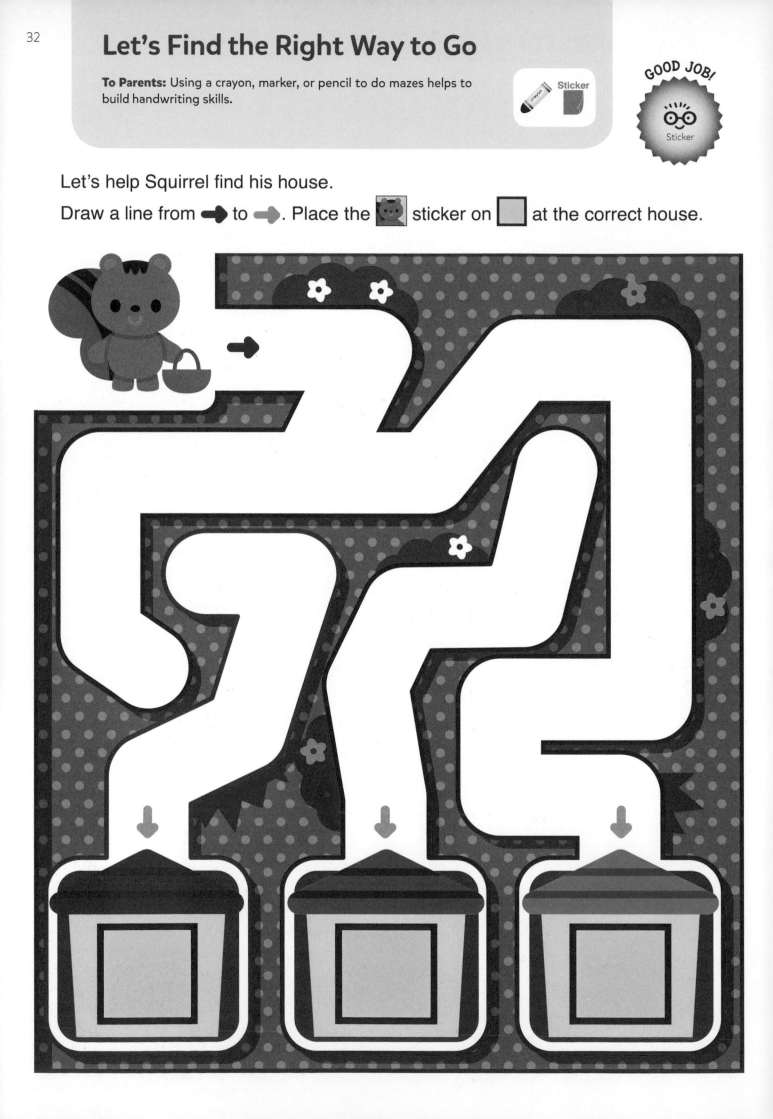

Let's Go Through the Maze

To Parents: Explain that there are obstacles to avoid in this maze. Your child should not draw over the vehicles. He or she should find another way around.

Let's help the animals get to the bakery. Draw a line from ➡ to ➡.

Find a path that is not blocked by vehicles.

34

Let's Go Through the Clouds

To Parents: Encourage your child to draw slowly to keep from bumping into the clouds. But it is okay if he or she goes outside the white area.

Oh, no! Elephant let go of the balloon.

Let's help Bird return the balloon. Draw a line from ➡ to ➡.

Let's Get Through the Maze

To Parents: This is a simple straight-line maze. Doing mazes helps children strengthen their fine motor skills and improve their ability to plan ahead.

Let's help Dog bring the ice pops to his friends before the ice pops melt.

Draw a line from ➡ to ➡.

Let's Fix the Broken Path

To Parents: Discuss how to correctly position the sticker so that it connects the broken part of the path. Have your child apply the sticker and then complete the maze.

Sticker / crayon

GOOD JOB!
Sticker

Let's help Piglet get home. Place the ▭ sticker on ⌐Sticker⌐.

Draw a line from ➡ to ➡.

Let's Fix the Maze

To Parents: Before your child applies the path sticker from the front of the book, discuss the importance of positioning the sticker correctly.

Sticker / crayon

GOOD JOB!
Sticker

Let's find out who Kitten is going to visit. Place the ▢▢ sticker on Sticker.
Draw a line from ➡ to ➡.

Let's Match the Animal Parts

To Parents: Here, your child will practice recognizing different parts of the same image and connecting parts of a whole.

Let's connect each head to the matching body.

Draw lines from ➡ to ➡.

Let's Match the Actions

To Parents: Start the activity by asking, "What do you do after you brush your teeth/wash your hair/wash your face?" Then, have your child connect each activity with what comes after.

GOOD JOB!

Sticker

Look at the children. What do you think they will do next?

Draw lines from ➡ to ➡.

40

Let's Go Through the Maze

To Parents: This is a color-coded maze. Have your child follow the path with red items. Then, ask your child to name the red items (cherries, tomato, apple).

GOOD JOB!

Sticker

Let's help Rabbit gather the red foods.

Draw a line from ➡ to ➡ by taking a path that has only red food.

Let's Follow the Food

To Parents: In this maze, your child will go from food to food. Ask him or her to name each object in the maze.

GOOD JOB!

Sticker

Let's help Bear find all the food.

Draw a line from ➡ to ➡ by taking a path that has only food.

Let's Complete the Maze

To Parents: This is a relatively complicated maze. Encourage your child to continue or start over if he or she comes to a dead end. Perseverance develops concentration skills.

GOOD JOB!

Sticker

Oh, no! Panda Bear is lost! Let's help him find his mother.

Draw a line from ➡ to ➡.

Let's Go Through the Maze

To Parents: Mazes train your child to look for possible problems or obstacles and then to find ways around them. They help to improve focus, problem-solving skills, and fine motor control.

GOOD JOB!

Sticker

Let's help Penguin find his friends by going over the bridges.

Draw a line from ➡ to ➡.

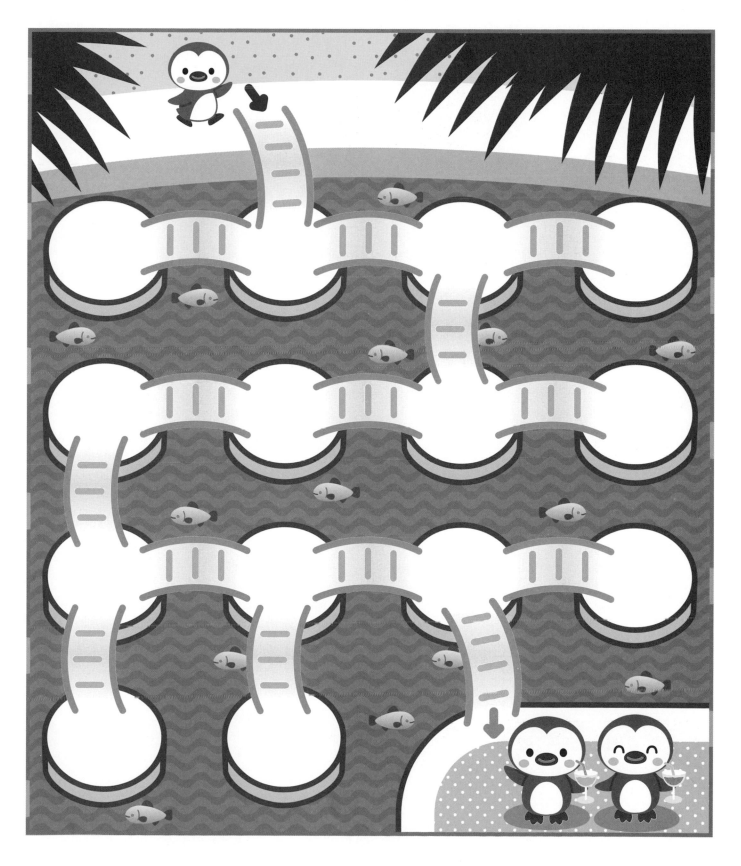

Let's Go Through the Maze

To Parents: Mazes help develop the ability to look ahead, spot future problems, and solve them.

GOOD JOB!

Sticker

Let's help Monkey get the balloon. Draw a line from ➡ to ➡.

Let's Color with Red

To Parents: After your child finishes coloring, ask him or her to name each object (fire engine, tomato, fish, crab, apple) to enhance his or her recognition skills.

GOOD JOB!
Sticker

Color all the objects red.

Let's Color with Yellow

To Parents: It is okay if your child colors outside the outlines. But you can always guide him or her to slow down and be more aware of each shape.

Color all the objects yellow.

Let's Color with Green

To Parents: Expand on the activity by asking your child to name the objects on the page and then saying, "What other things are green?" Have your child point to green items around the house.

Color all the objects green.

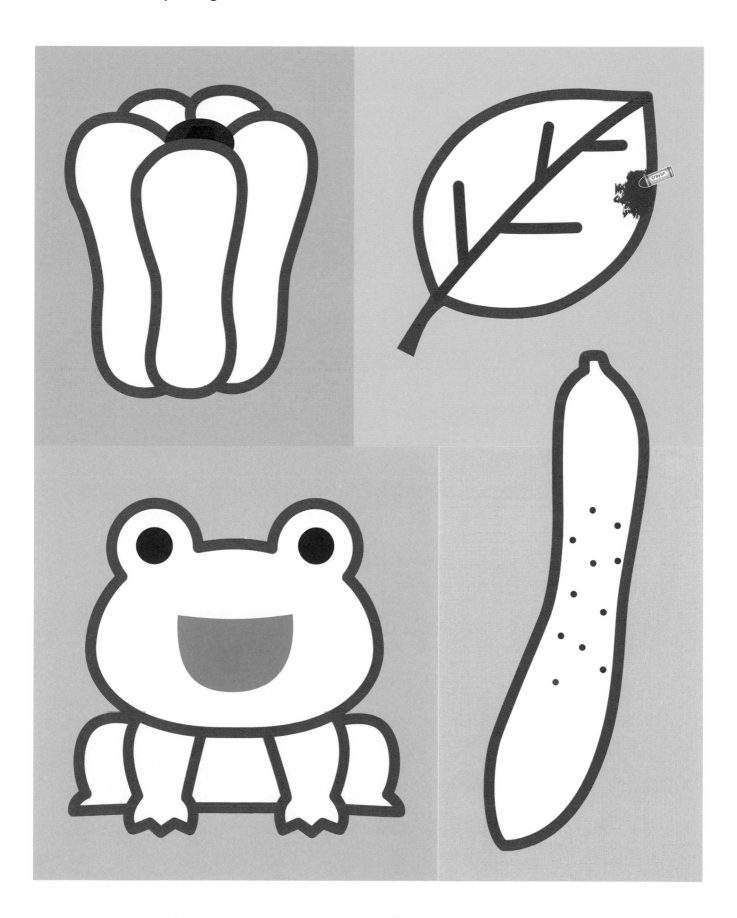

Let's Color the Bread

To Parents: Guide your child to choose the same colors (yellow, red) as the butter and jam in the picture.

Color with a yellow crayon to put butter on the bread.

Color with a red crayon to put jam on the bread.

Let's Color Breakfast

To Parents: Encourage your child to choose the same color as the outlines of each illustration. Ask your child to name the color she or he used for each food.

GOOD JOB!

Sticker

Color the egg yolks, sausage, and juice. Use a yellow crayon to color the egg yolks, a brown crayon to color the sausage, and an orange crayon to color the juice.

50

Let's Color the Orange

GOOD JOB!

Sticker

Trace the number with your finger. Then, color the orange.

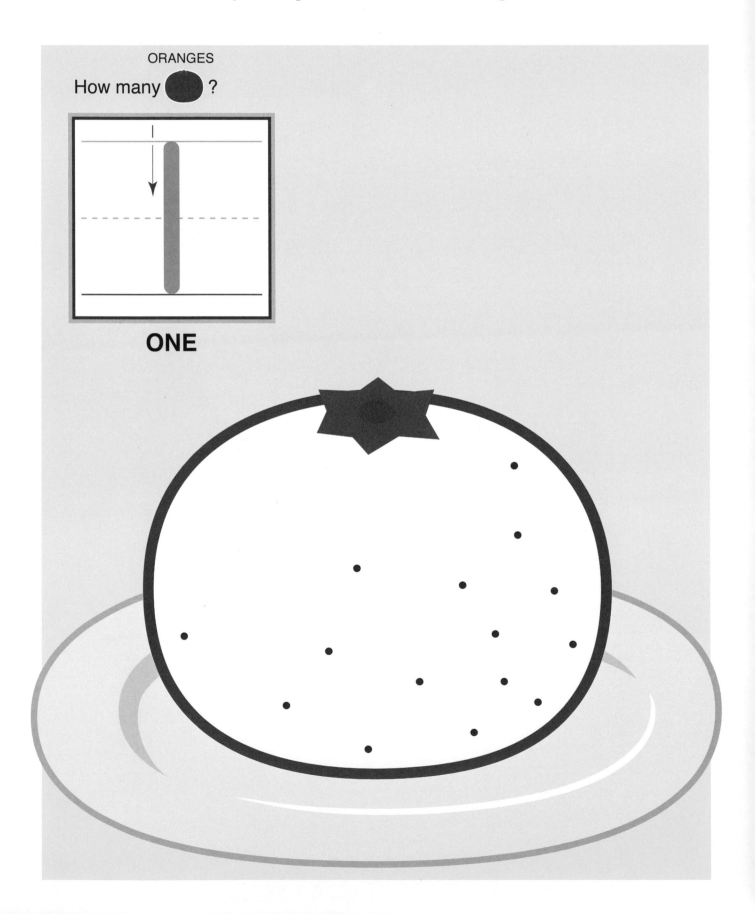

ORANGES

How many ?

ONE

Let's Color the Dolphins

To Parents: To improve your child's number recognition, ask, "How many dolphins are there?" Count, "One, two," while pointing to the dolphins.

Trace the number with your finger. Then, color the dolphins blue.

DOLPHINS

How many ?

2

TWO

Let's Color the Penguins

To Parents: By two years old, your child will likely understand the numbers one to three. By three or four years old, he or she will likely understand the numbers one through ten.

GOOD JOB!

Sticker

Trace the number with your finger. Then, color the penguin's nose and feet orange.

PENGUINS

How many ?

THREE

Let's Color the Balloons

To Parents: Use ordinary items in your home, such as shoes, toys, spoons, etc., to practice counting numbers and enhance your child's understanding.

GOOD JOB!

Sticker

Trace the number with your finger. Then, color the balloons. Use the crayon that matches the color of the outline of each balloon.

BALLOONS

How many ?

4

FOUR

Let's Connect the Dots

To Parents: As your child connects the dots, call out, "One, Two, Three, Four, Five." After your child connects the dots, a fox will appear. Help your child name the animal if he or she does not know what it is.

Draw a line by connecting each ● in order by number: 1, 2, 3, 4, 5.

What do you see? Color the animal brown.

Let's Draw Spots on a Cow

To Parents: It does not matter how many spots your child draws, but encourage her or him to keep them on the cow.

Draw spots on the cow.

Let's Draw Stripes on a Tiger

To Parents: Tell your child that a cow has spots and a tiger has stripes. Ask your child to name other animals that have spots or stripes (such as dogs, cats, zebras, etc.)

Draw stripes on the tiger.

Let's Draw Spots on a Giraffe

To Parents: Tell your child that each giraffe's pattern is unique. Say, "No giraffe has the same pattern as any other giraffe." Have your child compare the spots on the cow and the giraffe.

GOOD JOB!
Sticker

Draw spots on the giraffe.

Find the Matching Shapes

To Parents: After your child finishes coloring, ask, "What shape is the green building block?" Repeat with the other colors.

Find the building blocks with the same shapes. Then, color them to match.

Find the Shapes in the Doghouse

To Parents: To extend the learning, have your child look around your living room and find all the circles, triangles, and squares.

Find the ○, △, and □ in the picture. Draw over the outline of each shape with the same color as the dotted line.

Let's Draw Flowers

To Parents: Have your child draw flowers on the stems below. Say, "Use your imagination!" The flowers do not need to look realistic.

GOOD JOB!

Sticker

Draw flowers in any color.

Flower Garden

Let's Practice Cutting and Gluing

To Parents: Help your child cut out the king, prince, princess, and castle piece. Then have him or her place the cutouts correctly on the page before gluing them in place.

GOOD JOB!
Sticker

Cut out the picture shapes. Then, glue them onto the matching pink boxes in the picture below.

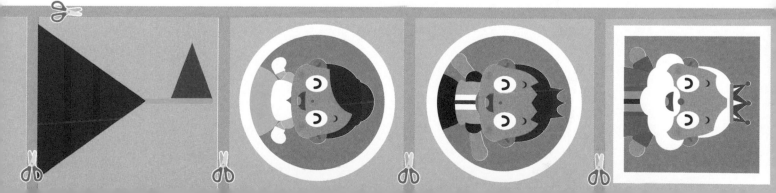

62

Let's Find the Animals

To Parents: After your child has drawn the lines, ask her or him to name the animals. Say, "Which animal is hiding behind the bush?" and "Which animal is hiding behind the cheese?"

GOOD JOB!
Sticker

Draw a line to connect each animal to where it is hiding.

Glue Glue Glue Glue

Let's See Who Is on the Boats

To Parents: Have your child pay special attention to each animal's unique characteristics (color, ear shape, etc.) Then, have your child use this information to decide which animal belongs on which boat.

GOOD JOB!

Sticker

The animals are having fun on the boats.

Cut the animals out. Then, glue them onto the matching boats.

Let's Greet the Teacher

To Parents: Encourage the use of proper greetings by asking your child, "When you see your teacher in the morning, what do you say?"

crayon

GOOD JOB!

Sticker

Draw a line to connect the matching words and pictures.

End of School Day

Beginning of Study Day

Hello

Good-bye

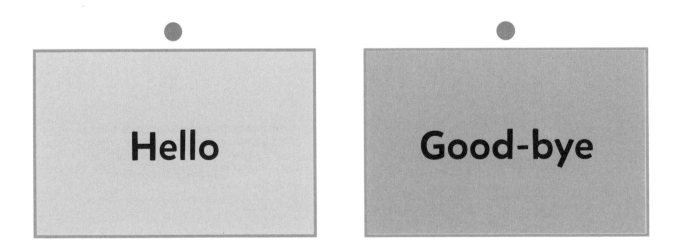

Glue   Glue   Glue   Glue   Glue